T0009525

PLANTPHABET

PLANTPHABET

A technicolour journey into the
secret world of indoor plants

Illustrations by Lynn Bremner

Harper *by* Design

A IS FOR
AIRBORNE

~~~

Air Plant

Air plants live in the air – it's as simple as that. Whether suspended from tree branches or clinging to rocks, they can be found in rainforests, swamps and even as high as the Andes mountain range.

Dracaena trifasciata

B IS FOR BREATHING

~

Snake Plant

Also known as 'mother-in-law's tongue', these plants excel at filtering indoor air. This makes them an ideal office buddy, but they're even better in a bedroom as overnight they convert most of the CO_2 into Oxygen.

C IS FOR

CASCADING

~~~~~

Wax Plant

Known for their thick, leathery foliage, wax plants are fast growers so feel free to prune if you want to keep them compact. Otherwise, show them off by wrapping their vines around a trellis or frame.

D IS FOR DELICIOUS

~~~

Cast Iron Plant

Native to Japan and China, the leaves and roots of this plant make a tasty snack for animals like deer and rabbits.

E IS FOR
ENORMOUS

~~~

Fiddle Leaf Fig

This is one of the most coveted of indoor plants due to the large, rough dark-green leaves that are shaped like a violin. It is perfect for homes with high ceilings but minimal floor space.

F IS FOR FANCY

~~~

String of Pearls

These little gems might resemble peas more than jewels, but their juicy, bead-like leaves are nothing short of impressive, especially when long strands are grouped or planted together.

G IS FOR GRACEFUL

~

Peace Lily

With dark, majestic leaves that arch outwards from soaring floral sails, this plant makes an eye-catching and uplifting addition to any home.

18

H IS FOR
HONEST

~~~~~

Heart Leaf

Who doesn't love a plant that tells you exactly what it needs? Yellow leaves mean you're overwatering, while brown means that it's time for a drink.

I IS FOR
ITCHY

~~~

Bunny Ears

Don't be fooled by the cartoon-cute
appearance and name of this
popular polka-dot succulent ...
one prick from the hair-like
spines can seriously
irritate your skin.

Opuntia microdasys

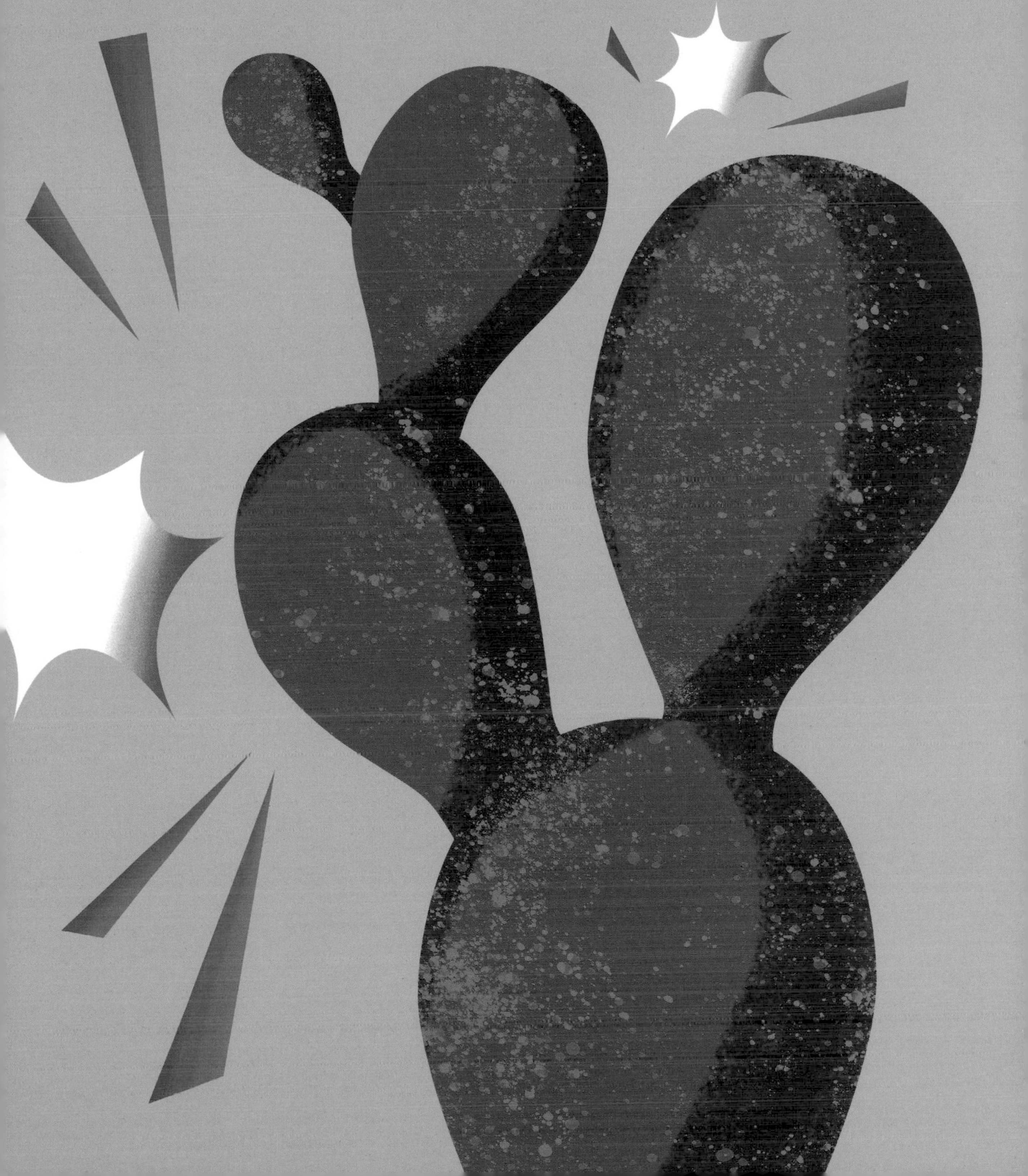

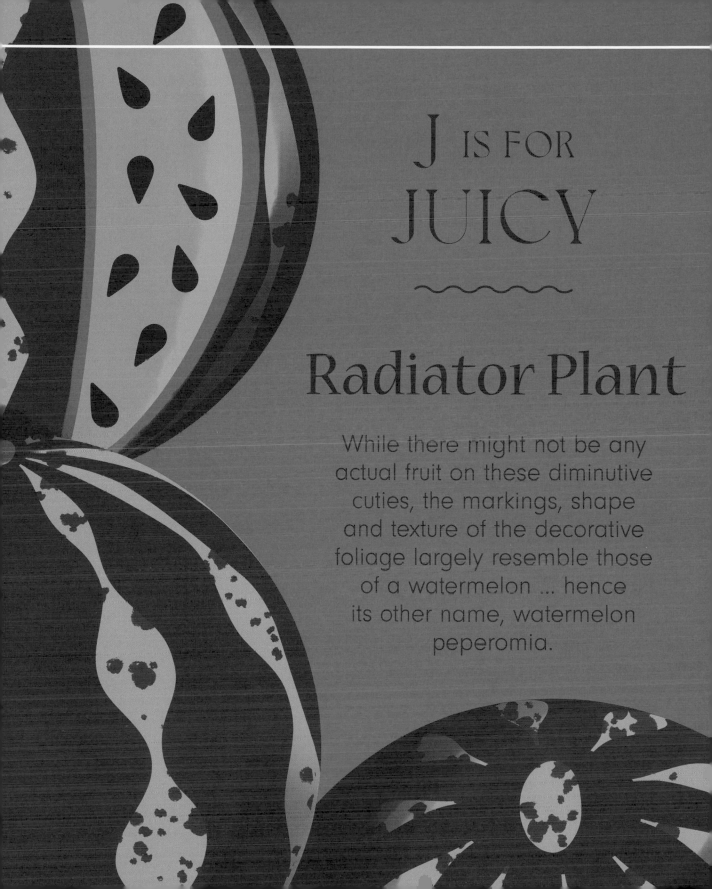

J IS FOR
JUICY

~~~

Radiator Plant

While there might not be any actual fruit on these diminutive cuties, the markings, shape and texture of the decorative foliage largely resemble those of a watermelon ... hence its other name, watermelon peperomia.

K IS FOR
KILLER

~~~

Chinese Evergreen

The leaves of this plant are often referred to as 'blades', which is fitting given that they produce poisonous crystals that can cause severe irritation and rashes.

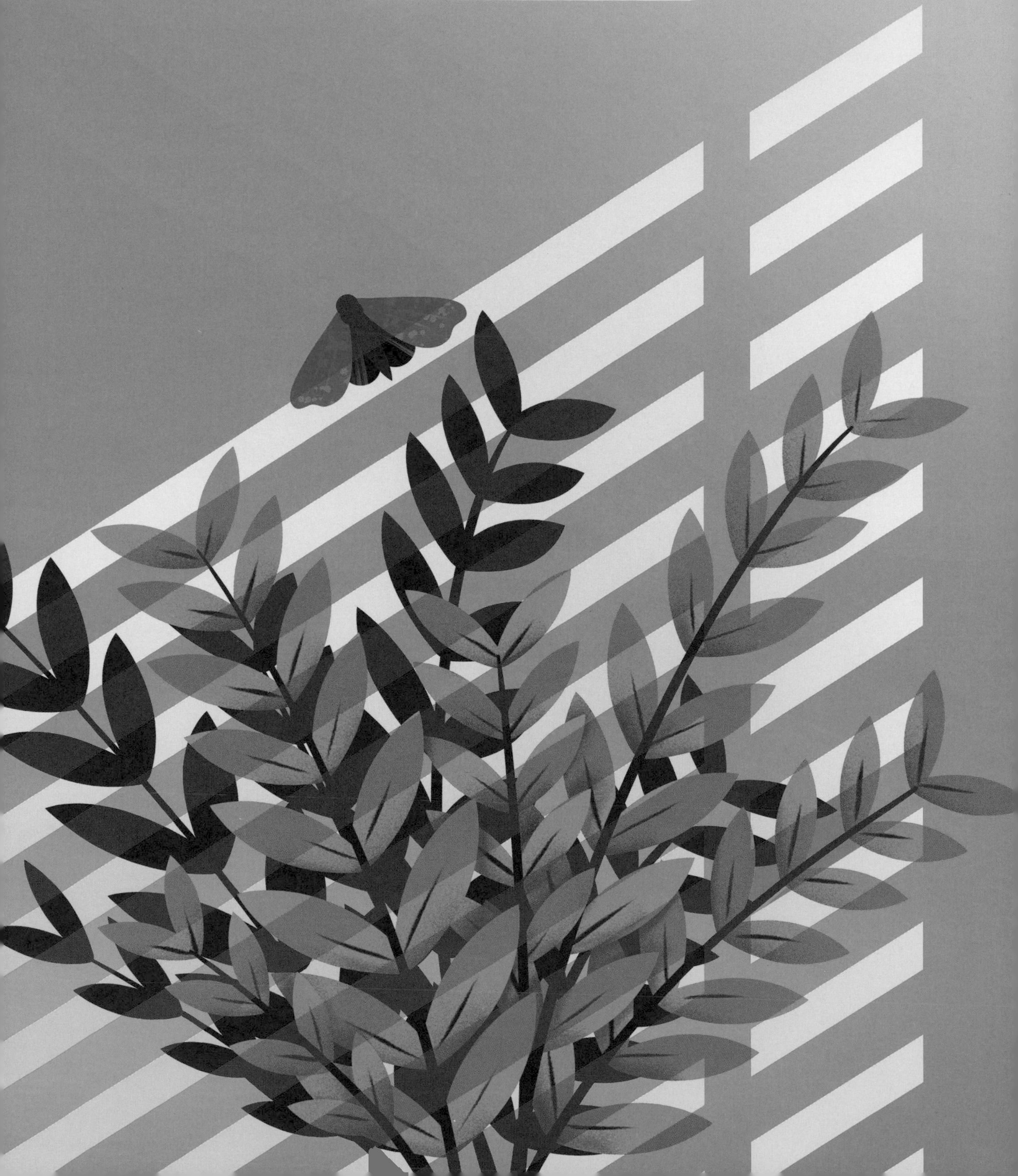

L IS FOR
LOW LIGHT

~~~

ZZ Plant

Ever wondered what houseplant would thrive in that windowless shoebox room in your home? This plant is the answer! It is tough and durable, and will grow even in the driest conditions or when neglected.

M IS FOR
MEDICINAL

~~~

Aloe vera

For centuries, Aloe vera gel has been widely used for its moisturising and healing properties. There are many commercial products available – you can even ingest the gel in smoothies – but it can also be used straight from the plant.

Aloe barbadensis

N IS FOR
NUMEROUS

~~~

Spider Plant

When cared for properly under the right conditions, the mother plant will rapidly reproduce many small 'daughters' at the ends of its long stems. Once these plantlets start to develop roots mid-air, they are ready to be removed and re-potted alone.

O IS FOR OTHER-WORLDLY

~~~

Chinese Money Plant

These plants are grown and adored for their unique circular foliage that resembles a coin, pancake or flying saucer. While not originating from outer space, they are universally popular on social media for their ornamental beauty.

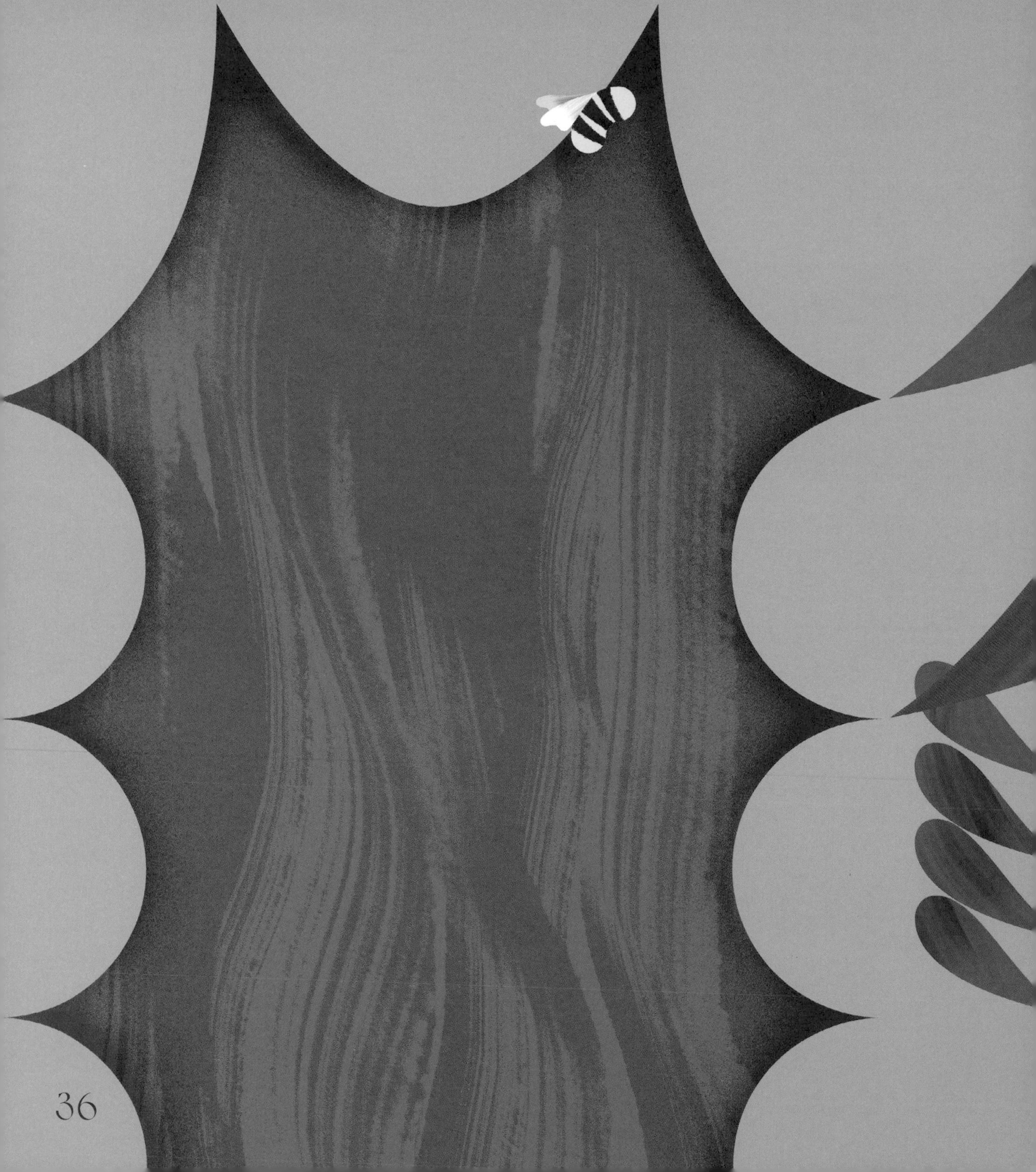

P IS FOR
PRICKLY

~~~

African Milk Tree

Also known as the cathedral cactus, this architectural beauty is covered with sharp, tiny thorns that grow from the three spines of each stem and can cause skin irritation.

Q IS FOR
QUIRKY

~~~~~

Prayer Plant

These striking plants fold up their leaves every night 'in prayer' and then unfurl them every morning in search of the sun. They do this with the help of an ingenious little joint between their stem and leaf.

R IS FOR
RESOURCEFUL

~~~

String of Hearts

There's a delicate romance that sometimes occurs in the natural world between plants and insects, in order to achieve pollination. The flowers on the string of hearts are adapted to form an umbrella-like canopy for flies to enter and help the process along.

S IS FOR SPEEDY

~~~

Devil's Ivy

This plant gets its common name because it is notoriously hard to kill. Under the right conditions, the trailing stems can quickly grow up to 2.5 metres (8 feet) in length, but it's wise to trim them back every now and then for fuller foliage.

T IS FOR
THIRSTY

~~~

Arrowhead Vine

When grown in a small pot,
these vines are particularly thirsty.
Mature plants require a solid
quenching several times a week
to make sure the soil remains moist.

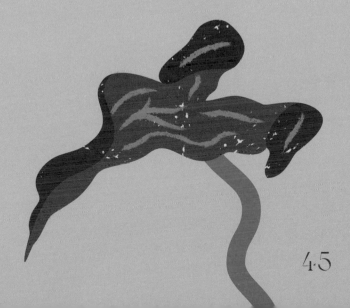

U IS FOR
UNFURLING

~~~

Swiss Cheese Plant

These tropical beauties grow super
fast under the right conditions.
One day you'll notice a
curled 'baby rosebud' and
the next, a brand new
leaf will emerge.

Monstera deliciosa

V IS FOR
VERTICAL

~~~

Dragon Tree

The only way is up for these slow-growing plants from Madagascar. They'll grow to 2 metres (6 feet) when indoors, but feel free to show them who's the 'Mother of Dragons' by pruning back any leaves that get too unruly.

W IS FOR WASP

~

Rubber Fig

Have you ever heard of a plant growing a fake fruit just to achieve pollination? Like other Ficus, it has a special symbiotic relationship with wasps, who are attracted to these poisonous (to people and pets), but fertile, fruits.

X IS FOR
X-RAY

~~~

Zebra Plant

The graphic markings on this plant might look more like set pieces from a Tim Burton film, but these exotic Brazilians are more 'Mardi Gras' than *Beetlejuice*, especially when in full bloom with radiant yellow flowers.

Y IS FOR
YAWNING

~~~

Bird's Nest Fern

With large, full fronds that yawn
out gracefully over one another,
and their distinctive wavy edges,
these plants make an impressive
addition to any indoor setting.

Z IS FOR
ZEN

~~~~~~

Lucky Bamboo

While it looks like it's part of
the bamboo family, this plant
is actually a herb. Its bunched,
twisted stalks make it a popular
choice for a calming bonsai
project as it is easily pruned
and shaped as desired.

PLANTPHABET NURSERY

Air Plant
Tillandsia

These plants don't have roots, and survive by absorbing water and nutrients through their leaves. They prefer full sun and environments with high humidity.

They thrive indoors in indirect light and do very well without much sunlight at all.

Snake Plant
Dracaena trifasciata

Wax Plant
Hoya carnosa

These plants like bright light, which will also help them flower. They can stand low temperatures, though not freezing, and like a sandy soil so the roots can drain and breathe.

Cast Iron Plant
Aspidistra elatior

While these might be a popular houseplant they also survive quite well outdoors in temperate climates down to −5°C and can withstand low light, low humidity and irregular watering.

These can grow quite tall (though not too bushy) and only need to be watered when the soil feels dry, so don't over-water.

Fiddle Leaf Fig
Ficus lyrata

String of Pearls
Senecio rowleyanus

These plants prefer a loose, sandy soil for fast drainage, and they don't need much watering during the winter months. They grow fast, so don't hold back on pruning stems as needed.

These low-maintenance beauties live best in shade with soil that is moist, but not too damp. They also grow well outdoors in a frost-free garden.

Peace Lily
Spathiphyllum

Heart Leaf
Philodendron hederaceum

Bright, indirect sunlight and well-drained, moist soil (with fertiliser once a month) will keep these super happy all year long.

Bunny Ears
Opuntia microdasys

These are native to the deserts of Mexico, so be sure to give them plenty of direct sunlight (except in winter when they hibernate) and only water when the sandy soil is dry to the touch.

Cool climate, bright light and not too much water will keep these plants happy. They also grow well as ground cover or grouped together with other plants in pots.

Radiator Plant
Peperomia argyreia

Chinese Evergreen
Aglaonema commutatum

These are low maintenance house plants that prefer low-light and cold conditions.

These grow slowly, but are easy to propagate from cuttings. While they hardly require any light to survive, a little love every now and then won't go astray.

ZZ Plant
Zamioculcas

Aloe Vera
Aloe barbadensis

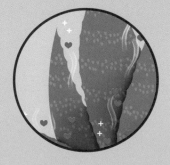

Like all succulents, these plants love bright full sun and sandy soil that drains easily. They don't need much water, especially in winter.

Spider Plant
Chlorophytum comosum

These plants prefer light and warmth, but cooler, darker spaces will slow the growth of reproduction if that's what you prefer. The soil should always be slightly damp during the warmer months.

These plants are in high demand, as they're slim, easy to grow and tolerate dry environments. They prefer bright, indirect light and benefit from regular rotation to maintain their shape.

Chinese Money Plant
Pilea peperomioides

African Milk Tree
Euphorbia trigona

These plants prefer draught-free, sunny conditions and a humid environment, like the bathroom. Make sure to let the soil dry out completely before watering.

These are among the trickier houseplants to care for. They prefer temperate climates, indirect, low light (they can burn quite easily) and soil that isn't too damp.

Prayer Plant
Calathea

String of Hearts
Ceropegia

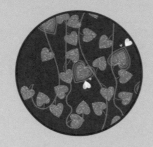

These plants can tend to look a little sad during the colder months, so don't water them too much. They do equally well in low or bright light and prefer soil suitable for succulents.

Although these will grow in low light, their leaves may become less variegated. They also grow well under fluorescent lights, making them ideal office plants.

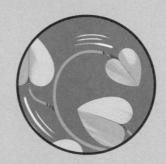

Devil's Ivy
Epipremnum aureum

Arrowhead Vine
Syngonium podophyllum

Native to tropical jungles, these vines prefer humid conditions over dry ones, which will make the leaves curl and brown. Some pruning is required to avoid them flopping over from excess weight.

These prefer bright, indirect light and humid conditions. Keep the soil moist in summer and dry in winter.

Swiss Cheese Plant
Monstera deliciosa

Dragon Tree
Dracaena marginata

These plants don't require a lot of watering or fertilising, especially in the cooler months. It's also good to avoid draughts as they can dry out the leaves.

Rubber Fig
Ficus elastica

~~~

These plants love humid, tropical and bright conditions, and a light misting of their leaves in summer.

These can be a little sensitive to water and light, so a general rule of thumb is not too much or too little of either. Err on the humid, bright, warm side of things.

Zebra Plant
Aphelandra squarrosa

~~~

Bird's Nest Fern
Asplenium nidus

~~~

As with most ferns, these prefer early/late indirect sunlight and humid, moist conditions ... just like the forest floor. Water the soil rather than the leaves as they are prone to mould and rot.

In summer, mist the leaves every day and keep these plants out of direct sunlight. They are equally at home growing in water or soil, but use purified water if possible.

Lucky Bamboo
Dracaena sanderiana

~~~

Harper *by* Design
An imprint of HarperCollins*Publishers*

HarperCollins*Publishers*
Australia • Brazil • Canada • France • Germany • Holland • Hungary
India • Italy • Japan • Mexico • New Zealand • Poland • Spain • Sweden
Switzerland • United Kingdom • United States of America

First published in Australia in 2022
by HarperCollins*Publishers* Australia Pty Limited
Level 13, 201 Elizabeth Street, Sydney NSW 2000
ABN 36 009 913 517
harpercollins.com.au

Copyright © HarperCollins*Publishers* Australia Pty Limited 2022

This work is copyright. Apart from any use as permitted under the *Copyright Act 1968*,
no part may be reproduced, copied, scanned, stored in a retrieval system, recorded, or transmitted,
in any form or by any means, without the prior written permission of the publisher.

A catalogue record for this book is available from the National Library of Australia

ISBN 978 1 4607 6060 4

Publisher: Mark Campbell
Publishing Director: Brigitta Doyle
Designer: Mietta Yans, HarperCollins Design Studio
Illustrator: Lynn Bremner
Printed and bound in China by RR Donnelley

8 7 6 5 4 3 2 1   22 23 24 25